What Is An Asthma Attack?

Carol Ballard

Raintree

Chicago, Illinois

www.heinemannraintree.com
Visit our website to find out
more information about
Heinemann-Raintree books.

To order:
☎ Phone 888-454-2279
▣ Visit www.heinemannraintree.com
to browse our catalog and order online.

© 2011 Raintree
an imprint of Capstone Global Library, LLC
Chicago, Illinois

Edited by Kate de Villiers and Vaarunika Dharmapala
Designed by Steve Mead
Illustrations by KJA-Artists.com
Picture research by Mica Brancic

Originated by Capstone Global Library Ltd
Printed in the United States of America by Worzalla
Publishing

15 14 13 12 11 10
10 9 8 7 6 5 4 3 2 1

Library of Congress Cataloging-in-Publication Data
Ballard, Carol.
  What is an asthma attack? : respiration / Carol Ballard.
    p. cm. — (Inside my body)
  Includes bibliographical references and index.
  ISBN 978-1-4109-4012-4 (hc) — ISBN 978-1-4109-
4023-0 (pb) 1. Respiration—Juvenile literature. 2.
Asthma—Juvenile literature. I. Title. II. Title: Respiration.
  QP121.B227 2011
  612.2—dc22   2010024675

Acknowledgments
The author and publisher are grateful to the following
for permission to reproduce copyright material: Alamy
pp. **5** (© David R. Frazier Photolibrary Inc.), **25** (© Radius
Images); Getty Images pp. **9** (FoodPix/Jupiterimages), **13**
(Photographer's Choice/Elyse Lewin); iStockphoto.com
pp. **18** (© Evelyn Peyton), **19** (© diego cervo), **20**
(© Thomas Eckstadt), **21** (© Lisa F. Young); Photolibrary
p. **16** (81A Productions); Science Photo Library pp. **7**
(Steve Gschmeissner), **10** (Custom Medical Stock Photo),
11 (Professors P. M. Motta & S. Correr), **14** (A J Photo),
17 (A J Photo), **22** (Jean Abitbol, ISM), **23** (Jean Abitbol,
ISM); Shutterstock pp. **4** (michaeljung), **15 band aid**
(© Isaac Marzioli), **15 gauze** (© Yurok), **21 band aid**
(© Isaac Marzioli), **21 gauze** (© Yurok), **27** (© Piotr
Marcinski).

Cover photograph of a boy holding an asthma inhaler
reproduced with permission of Science Photo Library
(Adam Gault).

We would like to thank David Wright for his invaluable
help in the preparation of this book.

Every effort has been made to contact copyright holders
of any material reproduced in this book. Any omissions
will be rectified in subsequent printings if notice is given
to the publisher.

Contents

Words that appear in the text in bold, **like this**, are explained in the glossary on page 30.

Why Do I Breathe?

Breathing is a very important process. To stay alive, you need to breathe. When you breathe, your body takes in air and gets rid of waste gas.

The air around us is a mixture of gases. Your body uses one of these gases, called **oxygen**. No matter what you are doing, your body needs oxygen. Without it, your body cannot maintain the basic processes that are needed for life. It cannot use the energy from your food.

No matter what you are doing, you need air to breathe!

On a cold day, you can see the air you breathe out as the water vapor in it condenses in the colder air.

Breathing in, breathing out

The more active you are, the more energy you use—and so the more oxygen your body needs. For example, when you run around, your muscles use a lot of energy, so they need a lot of oxygen. When you breathe in, air is sucked into your body. Your body takes the oxygen that it needs from this air.

Your body also produces a waste gas called **carbon dioxide** that it needs to get rid of. When you breathe out, the waste carbon dioxide is pushed out of your body and into the air around you.

Where Does the Air Go?

Air travels through a system of tubes in your head, neck, and chest called **airways**. Together, your lungs and airways make up the **respiratory system**. This has just one job: to get air into and out of your lungs.

🔍 **This diagram shows the respiratory system and where it is in your body.**

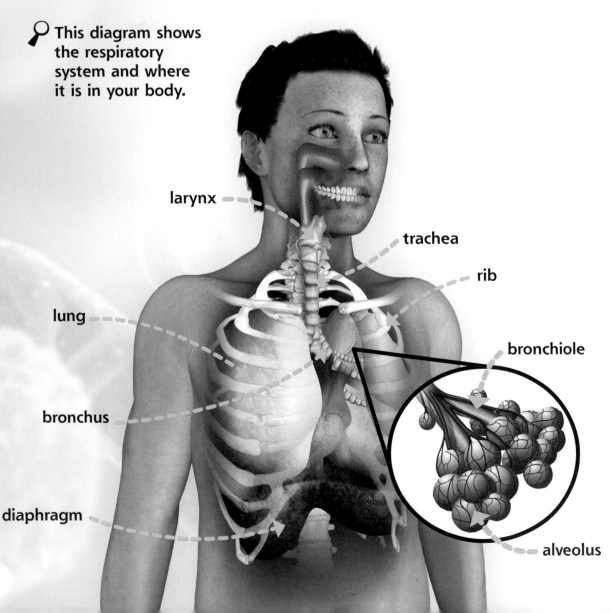

larynx

trachea

rib

lung

bronchiole

bronchus

diaphragm

alveolus

Air enters your body through your mouth or nose. The air travels down through your **larynx** and then continues down through your **trachea**.

Inside the lungs

The trachea divides into two branches, called the left and right **bronchi**. They take air into your left and right lungs. Each lung is like a spongy balloon that can fill with air and then empty.

Inside each lung, the bronchi divide again and again. These tubes, called bronchioles, get narrower and narrower. At the end of the bronchioles are clusters of tiny hollow balls called **alveoli**. Air is drawn into the alveoli when you breathe in, and it is pushed out of the alveoli when you breathe out.

🔍 **Mucus** inside your airways traps dust and dirt. Tiny hairs wave back and forth to move the mucus, dust, and dirt away from the lungs and up into the throat, where you swallow it.

What Happens When I Breathe In?

Ask a friend to hold a tape measure around your chest, under your arms. Breathe in deeply. Your friend should have to let the tape out a little. Can you feel your chest getting bigger? This helps to suck air into your lungs.

Your lungs are in your chest. They are protected by the bony cage of your ribs. All the ribs have muscles attached to them. These muscles can move the ribs up and down.

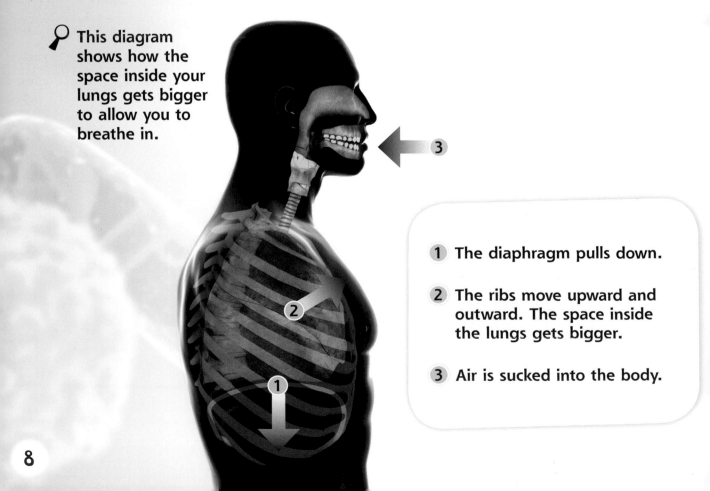

This diagram shows how the space inside your lungs gets bigger to allow you to breathe in.

1 **The diaphragm pulls down.**

2 **The ribs move upward and outward. The space inside the lungs gets bigger.**

3 **Air is sucked into the body.**

The diaphragm

Across the bottom of your chest is a sheet of stretchy muscle. This muscle is called the **diaphragm**. It can move up and down. When you need to breathe, your diaphragm pulls downward. The muscles between the ribs pull the ribs upward. Together these two actions increase the space inside your chest, and air is sucked in.

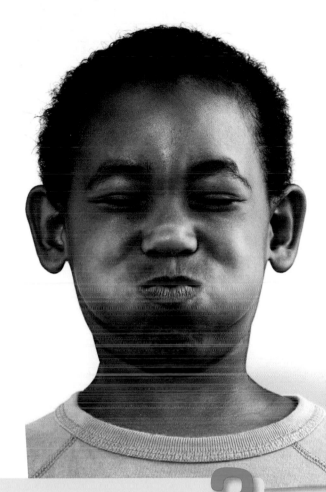

This boy is holding his breath to try to cure his hiccups.

SCIENCE BEHIND THE MYTH

MYTH: A scare can cure hiccups.

SCIENCE: Hiccups happen when the diaphragm jerks downward quickly. This disrupts your normal breathing rhythm, and air is sucked into your lungs really fast. The flap covering the top of your throat snaps shut with a "hic" sound.

The myth is true! A sudden scare can sometimes cure hiccups. As you think about something else for a second, your diaphragm has a chance to get back to its normal rhythm. Other remedies include sipping a glass of water slowly or holding your breath for as long as you can!

What Happens Inside My Lungs?

Two very important things happen inside your lungs:

1. Blood picks up the **oxygen** your body needs.
2. Blood gets rid of the **carbon dioxide** your body does not need.

Blood vessels

When you breathe in, air is sucked into your lungs through the **bronchi**. It reaches the **alveoli** at the end of the narrowest **airways**. Each alveolus is surrounded by a mesh of fine tubes, called **blood vessels**, through which blood flows. The blood vessels and the alveoli have very thin walls so that gases can pass through them.

This photograph shows the inside of a bronchus, one of the tubes through which air travels into and out of the lungs.

Red blood cells

Oxygen passes through the walls of the alveoli and the walls of the blood vessels. It gets picked up by **red blood cells** and carried away to different parts of the body.

At the same time, carbon dioxide moves out of the blood. It goes through the walls of the blood vessels and through the walls of the alveoli. It stays inside your lungs until you breathe out.

There are millions of red blood cells in a single drop of blood. This photograph has been magnified many times to show red blood cells inside a blood vessel.

What Happens When I Breathe Out?

Ask a friend to hold a tape measure around your chest, under your arms. Breathe out deeply. Your friend should have to pull the tape a little tighter. Can you feel your chest getting smaller? This helps to push air out of your lungs.

Breathing out is the opposite of breathing in. Your **diaphragm** pushes upward, and the muscles between the ribs pull the ribs downward. Together, these two actions make the space inside your chest smaller. Air is pushed out.

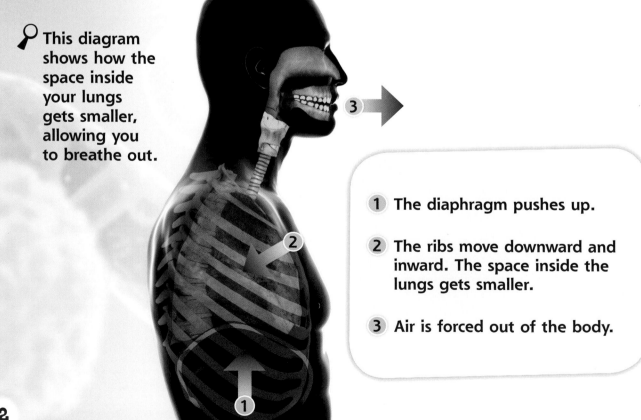

🔍 **This diagram shows how the space inside your lungs gets smaller, allowing you to breathe out.**

1 **The diaphragm pushes up.**

2 **The ribs move downward and inward. The space inside the lungs gets smaller.**

3 **Air is forced out of the body.**

Your breathing rhythm

Most of the time, you breathe in and out without even thinking about it. Sometimes, though, you need to control your breathing. For example, activities such as swimming, diving, singing, and playing wind instruments all need good breath control. When you stop your activity, your breathing rhythm goes back to normal.

Playing a wind instrument such as this flute takes good breath control—and lots of practice!

What Is an Asthma Attack?

Many people, both children and adults, suffer from **asthma**. It is a condition that makes it hard to breathe. If you have asthma, an attack probably makes you cough and wheeze. Your chest might feel tight, and you will almost certainly feel short of breath.

Things such as animal hair, some foods, air pollution, hay fever, or exercise can trigger asthma. If you know what triggers your asthma, it is a good idea to try to avoid it, so that you stay well and free of asthma attacks.

🔍 **Using an inhaler and sitting quietly for a few minutes will help to relieve this girl's asthma.**

What happens during an asthma attack?

When something triggers an asthma attack, the **airways** tighten and become narrower. The lining of the airways swells. Sticky **mucus** can build up, too, making the airways even narrower. This makes it very difficult to breathe.

Treating asthma

Most people who suffer from asthma control the problem by using an **inhaler**. When people use their inhalers, they inhale medicine. As it enters the airways, the medicine makes the airways relax and widen again.

Some inhalers prevent an asthma attack from occurring. Others relieve the symptoms of an attack. If you suffer from asthma, you should keep your inhaler with you at all times.

Practical advice

Handling an asthma attack

Asthma attacks can be a little scary. If you do have an asthma attack, try not to worry. Use your inhaler immediately. Stay calm and take deep, slow breaths. If you still feel bad, get an adult to help you or call a doctor.

How Much Air Can My Lungs Hold?

Different people's lungs hold different amounts of air. The bigger and fitter you are, the more air your lungs can hold. The amount of air your lungs can hold is called your lung capacity.

You can use a balloon to find out your lung capacity. Take the very deepest breath you can and then blow into the balloon. Stop when you feel you have squeezed out every last bit of air. Tie a knot in the neck of the balloon to stop the air from escaping.

Even after all that blowing, there is still about 1 liter (2 pints) of air left in your lungs that you simply cannot breathe out. Your lung capacity is all the air in the balloon plus that last liter!

Shallow breathing

Most of the time, we do not breathe in and out deeply. In normal, shallow breathing, only about a half a liter (1 pint) of air enters and leaves your lungs each time you breathe.

Testing lung function

Doctors use an instrument called a spirometer to measure the lung capacity of people who have difficulty breathing. The spirometer measures how much air moves into and out of the lungs, and how quickly this happens. This helps the doctor to find out how well the person's lungs are working.

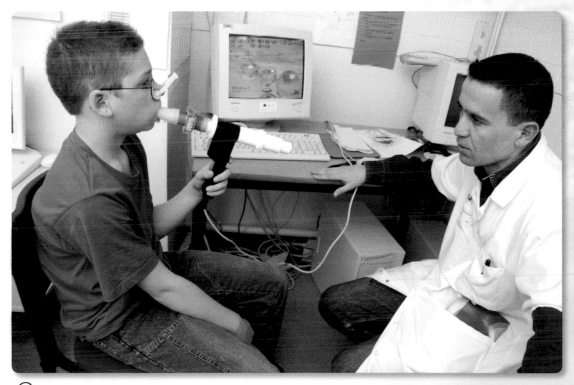

🔎 **This boy is using a spirometer to measure his lung capacity.**

Why Do I Get Out of Breath When I Run?

Your body needs **oxygen** every moment of every day and night. Oxygen helps your body to get energy from the food you eat. How much oxygen your body needs depends on what you are doing.

When you are asleep or resting, your body is using very little energy. This means it is not using much oxygen. Also, it is producing only a small amount of **carbon dioxide**. Breathing slowly is enough to get oxygen in and let carbon dioxide out.

🔍 **You breathe slowly when you are asleep.**

Moving around

When you start to move around, everything speeds up a little. Your body does more work, so it uses more energy. It needs more oxygen, and it produces more carbon dioxide. This means that you start to breathe more quickly.

🔍 **This girl is taking some quick, deep breaths after running fast.**

When you run really fast, your breathing has to speed up even more. If your lungs cannot supply as much oxygen as your muscles need, you have to stop and take a lot of breaths very quickly. This is what people call "getting out of breath." Taking a lot of breaths very quickly gets a lot of oxygen into your body. When you have enough oxygen, your breathing slows down and returns to its normal rate.

What Happens When I Cough?

We usually cough when something is irritating our **airways**. A cough can help to clear them out. Some things that irritate the airways are:

- **infections**, such as a cold
- conditions that affect breathing, such as **asthma**
- smoking, which damages the lungs
- substances in the air around you, such as smoke
- some medicines.

You should always cover your mouth when you cough to stops germs from spreading.

Coughing and choking

A cough starts when you take a deep breath in. This is followed by a breath out. As you breathe out, the **vocal cords** open and air is pushed out violently. At this point, you make the noise we call a cough.

Sometimes food gets into the airways. This can make the person cough violently over and over again. We call this violent coughing "choking." This usually clears away whatever was blocking the airways.

Practical advice

First aid for choking

If someone who is choking can still talk, his or her airway is only partly blocked. Air can still get in and out of the person's lungs. Sometimes hitting a choking person between the shoulder blades can help. If the person cannot talk, the airway may be completely blocked. You may need to call 911 for emergency help.

What Happens When I Talk?

Can you imagine what it would be like if you could not talk? How would you tell a friend a secret? Or answer a question in class? Have you ever wondered how we are able to talk?

When air enters and leaves the lungs, it passes through the **larynx**. This is where the **vocal cords** are.

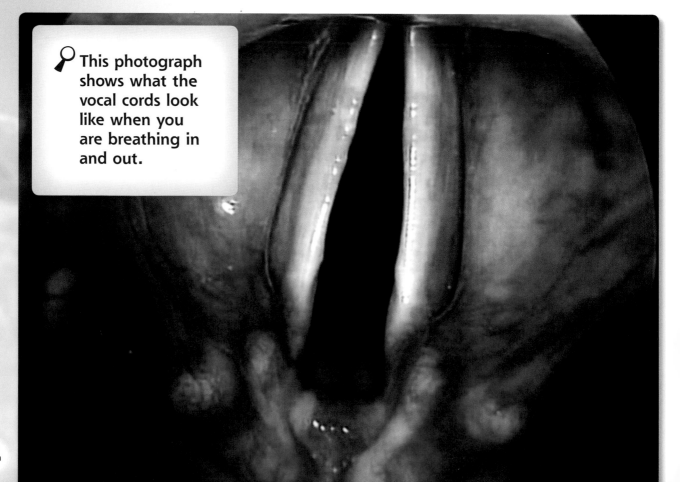

🔎 **This photograph shows what the vocal cords look like when you are breathing in and out.**

When you are breathing but not talking, there is a space between the vocal cords. Air can flow between them freely.

The voice

When you talk, the vocal cords are pulled to the center of the larynx. As you breathe out, the air rushing through them makes them **vibrate**. This makes the sound we call our "voice."

The vocal cords are kind of like strings on a guitar. A short, thin string makes a high sound, and a long, thick string makes a low sound. A man's larynx is larger than a woman's and his vocal cords are thicker. This is why men usually have deeper voices than women.

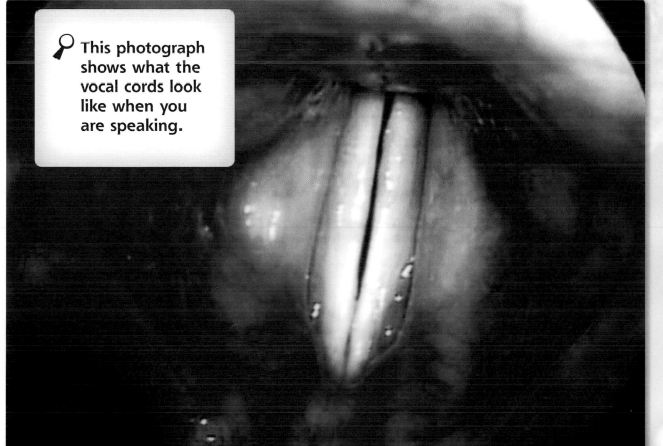

🔎 This photograph shows what the vocal cords look like when you are speaking.

How Can I Breathe Without Air?

What do you do if there is no air to breathe? You take your own **oxygen** supply with you! For people such as divers, firefighters, and astronauts, this is essential for survival.

Underwater

If you swim with your face just below the surface of the water, you can use a snorkel to breathe. This is a short pipe with a mouthpiece at one end. The other end stays above the water. This means you can breathe in and out normally through the snorkel pipe.

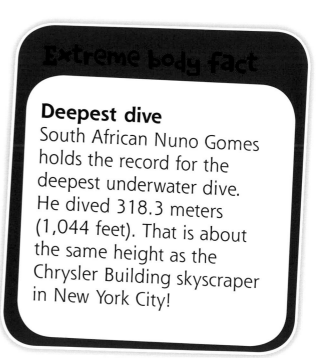

Extreme body fact

Deepest dive
South African Nuno Gomes holds the record for the deepest underwater dive. He dived 318.3 meters (1,044 feet). That is about the same height as the Chrysler Building skyscraper in New York City!

Some divers go deeper underwater, so they need to carry an air supply with them. They have a tank of air attached to their back. They breathe in and out through a tube that links the air supply with their mouth.

Firefighting

Firefighters often have to enter buildings that are filled with smoke or dangerous gases. This could choke them or damage their lungs. To avoid this, they carry an air supply and a face mask.

🔍 **Without an air supply, this firefighter would find it impossible to breathe in the smoke and flames.**

In space

There is no air in space. Spacecraft have life support systems, but if an astronaut has to go outside, he or she must take an oxygen supply. An astronaut wears a special space suit with an air supply strapped onto it.

How Can I Take Care of My Lungs?

Your lungs are very important. Without them you would not be able to breathe. Here are some ways in which you can take care of your lungs:

✔ Do not smoke. Tobacco smoke contains substances that damage the lungs. It makes them less stretchy, so they cannot take in as much air as normal. Tobacco smoke can also cause serious lung diseases.

✔ Avoid other people's smoke. If someone near you is smoking, the smoke does not just affect the smoker—you will breathe it in, too!

✔ Practice good hygiene. Washing your hands regularly can help you to avoid cough and cold germs. Use a tissue when you sneeze, and cover your mouth when you cough to prevent others from picking up your germs.

Asthma

If you suffer from **asthma**, there are some extra ways you can take care of your lungs:

- Try to avoid the things that trigger your asthma attacks.

- Wherever you are, whatever you are doing, keep your **inhaler** handy in case you have an asthma attack.

- Wherever you are, make sure that someone you are with knows you have asthma, so he or she can help you if you have an attack.

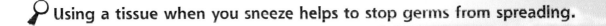 Using a tissue when you sneeze helps to stop germs from spreading.

All About Breathing

When running or jogging, breathe in a regular pattern. This will make you more comfortable, and you will be able to keep going for longer.

If you are feeling anxious or scared, sit still for a few minutes and take some slow, deep breaths. You will feel much better.

Take a breath!

Before lifting something heavy, take a breath in. Then breathe out while you are lifting. This will make the effort easier!

If you have been sitting in a stuffy room with not much **oxygen** in it, you may start yawning a lot. A yawn is like a big breath. It draws extra oxygen into your lungs.

Your respiratory system

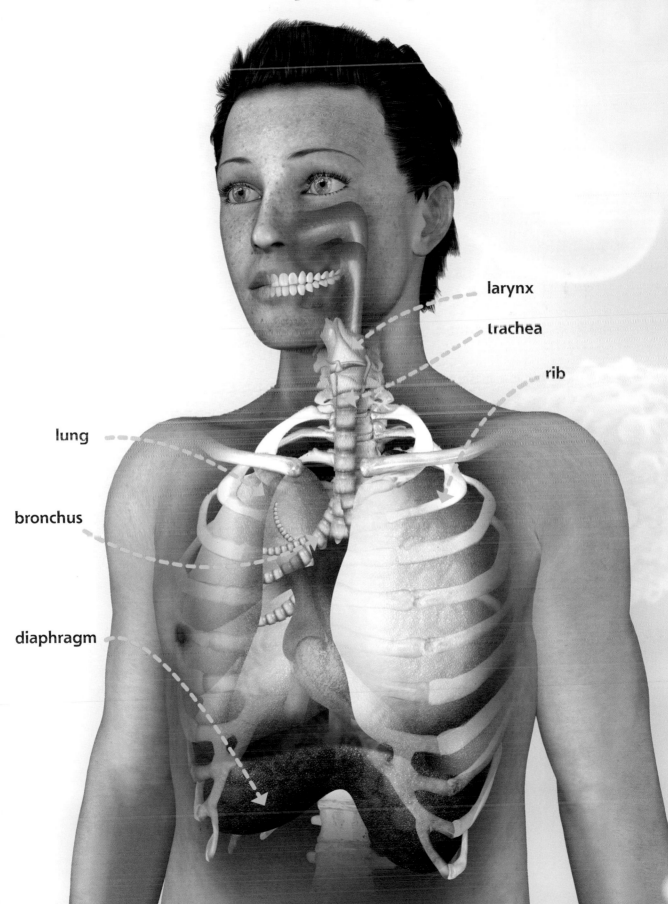

larynx

trachea

rib

lung

bronchus

diaphragm

Glossary

airway part through which air enters and leaves the body

alveolus (more than one: **alveoli**) part of the lung where oxygen enters the blood and carbon dioxide leaves the blood

asthma condition that can make a person cough, wheeze, and have difficulty breathing

blood vessel tube through which blood travels around the body

bronchus (more than one: **bronchi**) tube linking the trachea and the lungs

carbon dioxide waste gas made by the body

diaphragm sheet of muscle below the lungs

infection invasion of the body by germs that can cause diseases

inhaler device that contains medicine to prevent or relieve asthma

larynx part of the trachea where the vocal cords are

mucus sticky substance in the lining of the airways

oxygen gas that the body needs

red blood cell cell that carries oxygen around the body

respiratory system lungs and all the airways

trachea tube through which air passes between the mouth and lungs

vibrate when something shakes very fast, usually many times

vocal cord flap of skin that vibrates when you talk

Find Out More

Books

Levete, Sarah. *Understanding the Heart, Lungs, and Blood* (*Understanding the Human Body*). New York: Rosen, 2010.

Solway, Andrew. *Heart and Lungs* (*Your Body: Inside and Out*). Mankato, Minn.: Sea-to-Sea, 2011.

Spilsbury, Louise. *Respiration and Circulation* (*The Human Machine*). Chicago: Heinemann Library, 2008.

Websites

http://kidshealth.org/kid/htbw/lungs.html

Visit this website to learn more about the lungs and respiratory system. Check out a video of a breathing test.

http://science.nationalgeographic.com/science/health-and-human-body/human-body/lungs-article.html

Learn more about the lungs at this website, which is full of interactive features, including one on the effects of asthma.

www.starlight.org/asthma/

Play the "Quest for the Code" asthma game at this website. This fun site includes a 3D, interactive tour of the lungs.

Index